Summary and Analysis of

GUNS, GERMS, AND STEEL

The Fates of Human Societies

Based on the Book by Jared Diamond

WORTH BOOKS
SMART SUMMARIES

All rights reserved, including without limitation the right to reproduce this book or any portion thereof in any form or by any means, whether electronic or mechanical, now known or hereinafter invented, without the express written permission of the publisher.

This Worth Books book is based on the 2005 hardcover edition of *Guns, Germs, and Steel* by Jared Diamond published by W. W. Norton & Company.

Summary and analysis copyright © 2017 by Open Road Integrated Media, Inc.

ISBN 978-1-5040-4657-2

Worth Books
180 Maiden Lane
Suite 8A
New York, NY 10038
www.worthbooks.com

WORTH BOOKS
SMART SUMMARIES

Worth Books is a division of Open Road Integrated Media, Inc.

The summary and analysis in this book are meant to complement your reading experience and bring you closer to a great work of nonfiction. This book is not intended as a substitute for the work that it summarizes and analyzes, and it is not authorized, approved, licensed or endorsed by the work's author or publisher. Worth Books makes no representations or warranties with respect to the accuracy or completeness of the contents of this book.

Contents

Context

Jared Diamond wrote *Guns, Germs, and Steel* partly to refute familiar, racist explanations for the political and cultural dominance of European and Asian societies over others. According to Diamond, the old rhetoric of "civilized people" (usually Eurasians) versus "savages" (usually non-Eurasian indigenous peoples) was fallacious.

In a 2004 interview with PBS, the fundamental question Diamond was looking to address was "why history unfolded differently on the different continents over the last 13 thousand years."

In his search for the ultimate causes of Eurasian dominance, Diamond chose to focus on two often-overlooked areas of history: the history of non-

Eurasian native societies, and human history before 3000 BCE. The prehistory of indigenous societies, argued Diamond, can shed light on the deeper reasons for modern history's course. *Guns, Germs, and Steel*, published in 1997, offered a new perspective on human history, one that placed geography and ecology, rather than biology, at the forefront of human history.

The book has since been translated into more than twenty-five languages, has sold millions of copies, inspired a three-hour program produced by National Geographic and PBS, and won a Pulitzer Prize for general nonfiction.

With the success of this work, and his impressive decades-long background in research and academia, Jared Diamond is now revered by many as a thought leader beyond the spheres of societal evolution, anthropology, geology, and the history of innovation. He is a sought-after speaker who can be found addressing non-academic audiences from a variety of platforms, including TED Talks, the Long Now Foundation, Talks at Google, and at a diverse range of schools and institutions.

Overview

When Spanish conquistadors first came to the New World, they did not find empty wilderness: There were millions of people there, with distinct languages and cultures. The Spanish were vastly outnumbered and totally isolated; interlopers in a foreign place. When General Francisco Pizarro encountered the Inca emperor Atahuallpa in 1532, he was one of only 168 soldiers facing eighty thousand Inca warriors, deep within the Incan empire. Yet Pizarro and his forces managed to capture Atahuallpa and slaughter more than seven thousand Inca soldiers within hours of their meeting. And within one hundred years of Columbus' "discovery" of the New World in 1492, the vast empires of the Inca, Maya, and Aztec had collapsed, and the population of the Americas had plummeted by 95%.

The Spanish conquest of the Americas is a familiar story, one that's quite similar to collisions between colonial powers and native peoples throughout the modern world, from the Chinese invasion of Taiwan to the Dutch settlement of South Africa and the British annexation of Australia. Out of this broad historical pattern, Jared Diamond's *Guns, Germs, and Steel: The Fates of Human Societies* draws a series of questions: Why were the Spanish able to defeat the Inca, and the British rout the Aborigines? Why have Europeans and Asians historically triumphed over the indigenous people of other continents? Why weren't the Australians, Americans, and Africans the ones who colonized Europe?

The immediate causes of Eurasian victories seem obvious. Europeans and Asians had advanced weaponry, immunity to the diseases that decimated native populations, and metal technologies—the titular guns, germs, and steel—that the conquered peoples did not have. But as Diamond points out, this explanation often suggests an ugly underlying assumption: Europeans were inherently superior to the people they enslaved or exterminated, and European technological and political advantages were symptoms of their biological ascendancy. With *Guns, Germs, and Steel*, Diamond sets out to dismantle racist explanations for Eurasian dominance by following what he calls "chains of causation" to identify the ultimate causes of history's evolution—outcomes which, asserts Diamond, spring from determinants within human environments, not human biology.

The literal and figurative roots of Eurasian dominance lie in the Eurasian continent itself. After a sweeping tour of human evolutionary and migratory history, from the beginnings of *Homo sapiens* to the human migration to the Americas in 12,000 BCE, Diamond trains his focus on the Fertile Crescent, a region in southwestern Asia where humans established the first farming societies. In the 9th century BCE, the Fertile Crescent was home to a panoply of domesticable wild grasses and mammals in an abundance unparalleled on any other continent. (Eurasians domesticated cows, sheep, dogs, goats, and horses, whose wild ancestors were native to the continent; in the Americas, the alpaca was the only domesticable native animal—horses arrived later with the Spanish.) Through the gradual and largely accidental process of plant and animal domestication, Eurasians formed the first farming societies.

With farming came more food per square mile, and with more food came more people. High population density led to the establishment of strong leaders and social classes. Among these social classes were soldiers, artists, and bureaucrats, who were freed from the obligations of farming and could instead devote themselves to waging war, making art, and inventing new technologies. Because Eurasia's major axis runs east to west, adjacent regions enjoyed similar climates and growing seasons, which allowed crops and technology to diffuse out of the Fertile Crescent and across the continent—to western Europe, for instance, where food production never emerged independently.

The same ease of diffusion lies behind the spread of written language, which only a very few food-producing societies invented without getting the idea from somewhere else. Because the Eurasian continent facilitated it, Eurasian societies exchanged goods and ideas and built off the innovations of their neighbors. The Europeans' head starts on agriculture and writing were not a matter of innate genius, nor did they result from hard work or particularly receptive cultural attitudes. European societies advanced through the happenstance of Eurasian geography and ecology.

Similar coincidences of environment account for the ravaging spread of disease among the native peoples of Australia, parts of Africa, and the Americas. The most devastating human diseases of the modern world originated from domestic animal hosts: Smallpox, tuberculosis, and measles originated in cows, while influenza first appeared in pigs. The dense populations of agricultural societies also expedited the spread of epidemics—germs spread best in crowds.

Because many of the animals that might have been domesticated by the indigenous peoples of Africa, Australia, and America were hunted to extinction when early hunter-gatherers first migrated there, the natives of those continents never had a chance to develop immunity to animal-borne illnesses. Had there been domesticable animals on those continents, then native African, Australian, and American pathogens might have devastated European populations, making the European conquest difficult or impossible.

In a final series of case studies, Diamond applies his theory to several specific regions and societies, examining the myriad ways in which the geographic and ecological features of a particular environment shaped its native society. Drawing on a broad variety of disciplines—linguistics, evolutionary biology, anthropology, genetics, epidemiology, and all realms of history—Diamond examines the diverging developments of New Guineans, Australians, North American Indians, the Chinese, and the varied inhabitants of Africa, including the Bantu, Khoisan, and Pygmies. Where domesticable plant and animals species were few, and a north–south major axis like that of Africa and the Americas prevented the effective diffusion of crops and animals (because of extreme climatic variation along similar longitudes), the indigenous populations developed tools, agriculture, and stratified societies long after their Eurasian counter-parts—if they developed them at all. In many cases, the arrival of Europeans truncated the advancement of societies that Diamond believes would have likely developed food production, agriculture, and complex political structures despite the environmental obsta-cles they faced.

Diamond excavates the causes of European domi-nance as if history itself were an archeological site, treating the proximate causes of Eurasian domi-nance—guns, germs, and steel—as only the topmost layers, brushing them away to reveal the ultimate causes beneath. The triumphs and losses of human societies, Diamond argues, result from environ-mental happenstance, not biological ascendancy. The foundation of his theory is the literal bedrock of human history: Earth and its continents, with all of their variable climates, geographies, and ecologies.

Summary

Prologue: Yali's Question

Jared Diamond first confronted what would become the central inquiry of *Guns, Germs, and Steel* in 1972, while studying the evolution of birds in New Guinea. There, Diamond met Yali, a local politician who asked him why New Guinea's European colonizers developed technology and political structures that native New Guineans never developed. Expanding Yali's question beyond New Guinea, Diamond asks: Why did human development progress so differently on different continents?

In response to his own query, Diamond argues that environmental variations, not biological differences, are responsible for the varying rates of human development on different continents.

Part One: From Eden to Cajamarca

A broad overview of human history, including two specific object lessons in geography and ecology's important roles in shaping the development of human societies.

Chapter One: Up to the Starting Line

Seven million years ago, human history began: A population of African apes diverged into three groups, one of which evolved into *Homo sapiens.*

Fifty thousand years ago, modern humans began to migrate out of Africa. They spread first to Eurasia, then to Australia and New Guinea, and finally to the Americas in 12,000 BCE. The arrival of humans to all continents except Eurasia coincided with the extinction of large native mammals. This left native Australians, New Guineans, and Americans without any large mammals—which would have serious consequences for their ancestors thousands of years in the future.

Chapter Two: A Natural Experiment of History

The Maori and the Moriori tribes descended from the same Polynesian ancestors sometime around 1200 CE. But in 1835, the Maori invaded the Moriori and slaughtered them with superior weapons, effective military organization, and advanced watercraft.

How did two branches of the same ancestral group become so different in so little time? The Maori were warrior-farmers who lived in fierce competition with other tribes in Northern New Zealand, while the Moriori were hunter-gatherers who lived and worked in communal harmony on the isolated Chatham Islands.

Chapter Three: Collision at Cajamarca

On November 16, 1532, General Francisco Pizarro met the Inca emperor Atahuallpa in the Inca city of Cajamarca. Though Pizarro's forces were vastly outnumbered, they were able to capture Atahuallpa and kill thousands of Inca without the loss of a single conquistador. Their unlikely triumph arose from a few advantages they had over the Inca: steel weapons, horses for transport, immunity to animal-borne diseases that had already killed many Inca, and a literate tradition that allowed them to make informed military decisions based on past precedent.

Part Two: The Rise and Spread of Food Production

In six chapters, Diamond identifies the ultimate causes of Eurasians' dominance over other continents. The most fundamental of these is agriculture. Food production is a prerequisite to complex, technologically advanced, and militarily dominant societies.

Chapter Four: Farmer Power

From the very start of human history, there were more plants and animals that humans could use in Eurasia than anywhere else. Because plants and animals were readily available there, but scarce on other continents, food production arose in Eurasia first. Agriculture supported larger societies, and larger societies became politically complex and technologically innovative. Plus, the domesticated animals of Eurasian societies transmitted the diseases they carried to their human handlers, which meant over time that Eurasians developed immunity to those diseases.

Chapter Five: History's Haves and Have-nots

Different societies developed food production at different times—and some societies never organized their food production at all. Agriculture was most likely developed independently in only a few places and at various times, from 8000 BCE in Southwest Asia to 3500 BCE in Mesoamerica. Elsewhere, societies did not develop agriculture even in ecologically suitable regions.

Most societies adopted crops, animals, and agricultural techniques from their neighbors. Egypt, for example, was probably introduced to new plants and farming methods from the Fertile Crescent in Southwest Asia.

Chapter Six: To Farm or Not to Farm

No society simply decided to become farmers instead of hunter-gatherers. The evolution was gradual, often due to geographic reasons, such as the availability of food per square mile, access to wild game, and better tools.

Farming and hunting-gathering represent two alternative and competing strategies for sustaining a population of people. In most cases throughout history, hunter-gatherers became farmers because they were forced to: they had to farm, or else be forced out of their land by farmers. Hunter-gatherer societies that avoided farming into modern times did so because they were confined to areas not suitable for food production.

Chapter Seven: How to Make an Almond

Plant domestication is the process of gradually making a wild plant more useful to humans. Wild almonds, for example, are bitter and contain lethal levels of cyanide. But sometimes, wild almond trees have a genetic mutation that makes their almonds tasty and safe for humans. Ancient people didn't gather non-bitter almonds intending to plant them—they chose the almonds that tasted best. When they discarded or accidentally dropped a few of the almonds they'd picked, they unconsciously promoted the growth of new almond trees bearing non-bitter almonds.

Domestication was a piecemeal, accidental, and self-catalytic process: the more people selected plants with certain desirable traits, the more plants with those traits grew, which meant more desirable food for those people, who could then grow in numbers and population density because of the availability of food.

Chapter Eight: Apples or Indians

Some plants are easier to domesticate than others, and those easily domesticable plants are concentrated in Southwest Asia and Europe. Many species of domesticable animals, including pigs, sheep, and cows, are also native to Eurasia.

In contrast, most of the plants native to the United States, New Guinea, and Australia weren't easy to domesticate—apple trees, for example, are genetically complex and slow-growing, making them hard to domesticate. As a result, food production arose later or not at all in those regions.

Chapter Nine: Zebras, Unhappy Marriages, and the Anna Karenina Principle

"Domesticable animals are all alike; every undomesticable animal is undomesticable in its own way," writes Diamond at the start of this chapter. According to his "Anna Karenina principle," domesticable animals all share key characteristics: they aren't picky eaters, they grow to maturity quickly, they reproduce in captivity, and they are submissive to humans. If an animal species lacks any single one of those characteristics, it cannot be domesticated.

Many domesticable animals were native to Southwest Asia and Europe. In Australia and the Americas, there were very few suitable native species, because most of the potentially domesticable animals native to those continents were hunted to extinction by early hunter-gatherers (as we learned in Chapter One).

Chapter Ten: Spacious Skies and Tilted Axes

The major axis of Eurasia runs east–west, which means that many societies in Eurasia exist along the same latitude, and so enjoy similar growing seasons and climates. Plants, domestic animals, and technologies (such as agriculture) readily diffused both eastward and westward across the Eurasian continent.

The major axes of Africa and the Americas run north–south. On those continents, there is a wild diversity of climate, hours of sunlight in a day, and seasons along the same longitudinal line. The north–south axes resulted in slow, difficult diffusion of ideas and technology across the Americas and Africa.

Part Three: From Food to Guns, Germs, and Steel

Now that he has detailed the ultimate causes of Eurasians' advantage over other peoples, Diamond traces the connections between ultimate and proximate causes, which include disease immunity, written language, technology, and political centralization.

Chapter Eleven: Lethal Gift of Livestock

Many of the most devastating human diseases in history started out infecting animals before making the jump to humans. Those who lived in close proximity to animals gradually developed immunity to the diseases they caught from animals. But people without many domesticated animals, like Native Americans and Australians, did not develop immunity to animal-borne diseases. As a result, Old World pathogens proved devastating to New World societies, but not vice versa.

Chapter Twelve: Blueprints and Borrowed Letters

Why did some societies develop writing, while others did not? Writing only developed independently in a few places: Sumer, Mexico, and possibly China and Egypt. In every case, writing seems to have arisen first as a way to keep track of stored food, goods, and trade. Writing was another corollary of food production.

Most societies that developed writing got the idea from one of those original sites of written language instead of coming up with an alphabet de novo. Societies that interacted with other groups often—such as those on the Eurasian continent—adopted written language long before more isolated societies.

Chapter Thirteen: Necessity's Mother

"Invention is the mother of necessity," writes Diamond. Great innovations, such as the wheel and iron tools came about only in food producing societies with the resources and population densities to support many inventors. Large, prosperous societies led to innovations, not the other way around.

In Eurasia, where societies lived in close competition with each other, and ideas easily passed from one group to the next, people built on each other's innovations and drove development forward in a self-catalyzing process.

Chapter Fourteen: From Egalitarianism to Kleptocracy

We can organize human societies in order of ascending complexity: tribes, bands, chiefdoms, states. Complex societies are food-producing societies—agriculture leads to dense populations, and dense populations lead to stratified social structures and strong leadership.

Political centralization can solve some of the problems that arise in denser societies, which include conflicts, resource allocation problems, space constrictions, and disputes with other tribes. These states can also effectively invade and conquer other tribes, chiefdoms, or states, and thereby expand.

Part Four: Around the World in Five Chapters

These five chapters apply the ideas developed in the preceding chapters to each of the continents and a few islands.

Chapter Fifteen: Yali's People

When Europeans arrived in Australia and New Guinea, they found what seemed like Stone Age tribes. Native Australians and New Guineans had no written language, little agriculture, and they still used stone tools.

Why? The extreme environments of New Guinea and Australia inhibited the development of agriculture. Neither region had sufficient native domesticable plants or animals to make farming competitive with hunting and gathering, except in the New Guinean highlands.

Chapter Sixteen: How China Became Chinese

China became unified in 221 BC. Diamond uses glottochronology to track the movement of agriculture, written language, and technological innovations through ancient China. The rise of food production in North China spawned a prehistoric movement of human population, language, and agriculture from North China into South China. This caused the entirety of China to become unified, as it has remained almost without exception ever since.

Chapter Seventeen: Speedboat to Polynesia

Diamond jumps back more than one thousand years, to what he believes was the start of an Austronesian expansion from South China through Southeast Asia, the Philippines, Indonesia, and all the way to the Polynesian Islands. However, the Austronesians were unable to colonize New Guinea and Australia.

Chapter Eighteen: Hemispheres Colliding

We return to the collision at Cajamarca between Pizarro and the Inca emperor Atahuallpa. We can see now that Pizarro's victory over Atahuallpa—and, by extension, Europe's conquest of the Americas—was the culmination of two separate historical trajectories that determined thousands of years previously by environmental differences between Eurasia and the Americas.

Chapter Nineteen: How Africa Became Black

Though Europeans colonized Africa as they did the Americas, the history of the African continent contrasts with that of the Americas. Africa has a different climate, and within its bounds are a hugely varied number of languages and peoples. With the exception of South Africa, European conquest did not lead to widespread or long-lasting European colonies in sub-Saharan Africa.

Diamond provides a sweeping overview of African human history, focusing especially on the prehistoric expansion of the Bantu people throughout the continent. The Bantu were an agricultural society that had the advantage over the hunter-gatherers they displaced throughout the sub-Saharan region.

Despite Africa's long pre-history, its scarcity of domesticable plants and animals and its north–south primary axis prevented most African societies from developing the guns, germs and steel that Eurasian invaders possessed.

Epilogue: The Future of Human History as a Science

In the final pages of his book, Diamond summarizes his argument: differences in continental geography and ecology led to differences in native peoples' historical outcomes.

By happenstance, Eurasians inherited an environment replete with domesticable plants and animals. They also happened to find themselves on a continent with an east–west axis, which allowed for relative ease of communication between peoples, and the knowledge of new technologies and agricultural methods to be shared from one society to the next.

Though much of prehistory is still unknown and potentially unknowable, Diamond champions human history as a science. Its methodologies may be different from chemistry or physics, but history's "natural experiments" are valuable subjects of study. Broad historical patterns are discernible, and they can teach us much about ourselves—our past, our present, and our future.

Timeline

4–1.7 million years ago: Three proto-human species—*Australopithecus africanus, Homo habilis*, and *Homo erectus*—split off from a common ape ancestor.

50,000 years ago: A period of rapid human development, which Diamond terms "The Great Leap Forward," begins. Humans begin to use stone tools, live in tribes, and create jewelry and artwork. Bands of humans start migrating from Africa across the globe.

40,000 years ago: Modern humans (also called Cro-Magnons) migrate into Europe, where they displace Neanderthals. There is no evidence of Neanderthals after this period.

40,000–30,000 years ago: Humans populate New Guinea and Australia. Human arrival coincides with the extinction of large native mammals.

11,000 BCE: Humans expand throughout the Americas. There, as in New Guinea and Australia, human arrival coincides with the mass extinction of large native mammals. Humans begin to live in villages.

9000–6000 BCE: Humans in the Fertile Crescent domesticate the first plants and animals, and subsequently begin to establish settled farming communities.

3500 BCE: Agriculture is invented in Mesoamerica.

3200 BCE: Written language first appears in the Fertile Crescent.

1300 BCE: The Chinese invent a written language.

900 BCE: The first iron tools come into widespread use in the Fertile Crescent.

1 CE: Andes Native Americans form a large, politically centralized empire.

600 CE: Writing appears in Mexico.

221 CE: China first becomes unified linguistically, culturally, and politically.

1492 CE: Christopher Columbus sails to the Caribbean, where he meets—and clashes with—the indigenous populations of the islands.

Please note that the dates in this timeline are approximate.

Direct Quotes & Analysis

"History followed different courses for different peoples because of differences among peoples' environments, not because of biological differences among people themselves."

This quote from the prologue offers a concise summary of the book's thesis. The following pages of *Guns, Germs, and Steel* are devoted to the explanation and exploration of this central proposition.

"Peoples of northern Europe contributed nothing of fundamental importance to Eurasian civilization until the last thousand years; they simply had the good luck to live at a geographic location where they were likely

to receive advances (such as agriculture, wheels, writing, and metallurgy) developed in warmer parts of Eurasia."

There's nothing inherently special about northern Europeans, according to Diamond. They do not possess more natural ingenuity, more tenacity, or better genes than other people. Eurasians simply inherited an advantageous environment, where they could easily receive and adopt the technologies and crops that the people of other parts of Europe invented; it is geography that led to specific advances for the Europeans. In this section, theories about the influence of human genetics and climate (a cold environment versus a tropical one) are dispelled.

"Much of human history has consisted of unequal conflicts between the haves and the have-nots: between peoples with farmer power and those without it, or between those who acquired it at different times."

Farming is the foundation of human development—when it comes to human history, farmers have the food, the weapons, the military, and the technology. And all of these assets enable trade and the potential for commercial wealth, of course. Historically, farmers had power—especially over those peoples who did not farm, or who began to farm later in their histories.

"Rhino-mounted Bantu shock troops could have over-thrown the Roman Empire. It never happened."

This quote illustrates the *"Anna Karenina* principle," which dictates that animals must possess a particular confluence of characteristics for humans to domesticate them. Rhinos have never been domesticated, even into the modern era, because of their aggression and their inability to submit to human commands. The Bantu, like many indigenous populations in Africa, Australia, and the Americas, had few suitable candidates for domestication available to them.

"In short, Europe's colonization of Africa had nothing to do with differences between European and African peoples themselves, as white racists assume. Rather, it was due to accidents of geography and bio-geography—in particular, to the continents' different areas, axes, and suites of wild plant and animal species."

Racist explanations for Africans' inability to fight off European colonizers—many of them familiar to the average English-speaking reader—typically suggest that physical differences between Africans and Europeans led to the Africans' defeat. In Chapter Nineteen, Diamond applies the principles of his environment-focused thesis to the specific path of African history. He finds that the continent's environment, not its people, caused history to unfold as it did in Africa.

Trivia

1. Spanish conquistador Francisco Pizarro held the Inca emperor Atahuallpa captive for eight months. Pizarro demanded a ransom for Atahuallpa's release. The Incas paid Pizarro nearly twenty-four tons of gold and silver—but when Pizarro received the ransom, he executed Atahuallpa anyway.

2. Only a dozen species—almost all of them native to the Fertile Crescent in Eurasia—account for 80% of the modern world's annual crop production.

3. Ethiopian farmers were the first people in the world to domesticate the wild coffee plant.

4. The region of New Guinea and the islands surrounding it has the highest concentration of languages in the world. More than one thousand of the world's six thousand languages are spoken there, all in an area only a slightly bigger than the state of Texas.

5. The first preserved example of Greek writing appears on a wine jug dating from around 740 BCE. The inscription reads: "Whoever of all dancers performs most nimbly will win this vase as a prize."

6. The Sahara wasn't always a vast desert. Between around 9000 BCE and 4000 BCE, the Sahara was a lush, grassy area fed by a large river system and inhabited by ancient people who raised cattle, sheep, and goats.

7. Author Jared Diamond earned a BA from Harvard College and a PhD in physiology from the University of Cambridge before arriving in New Guinea in 1964 when he decided to pursue the study of ecology and evolutionary biology.

8. The so-called QWERTY keyboard was invented in 1873 and designed specifically to make typists type slowly. According to Diamond, manufacturers used "anti-engineering" in their technology by placing the most common letters all over the keyboard to keep adjacent keys from jamming. More than a hundred years later, millions of users have kept the keyboard from evolving.

9. Domesticated or sweet almonds are delicious and nutritious, but eating too many wild almonds can kill you. Bitter almonds contain high levels of cyanide.

10. Russia's Cyrillic alphabet was derived by adapting Greek and Hebrew letters by Greek missionary Saint Cyril in the 9th century AD.

What's That Word?

Acculturate: Assimilate or cause to be assimilated to another culture, usually the dominant culture.

Anna Karenina principle: A notion developed by Jared Diamond and sometimes applied in the discipline of statistics, this rule suggests that failure in an endeavor can be caused by a number of factors, but in order to achieve success all of those necessary factors must be present. This principle alludes to the opening line of Leo Tolstoy's masterwork Anna Karenina: "Happy families are all alike; every unhappy family is unhappy in its own way." Diamond uses this in the discussion of domestication.

Clovis theory: The hypothesis that the Clovis people, named after the New Mexico town where their artifacts were first discovered, were the first inhabitants of the Americas around 12,000 BCE.

De novo: Starting from the beginning; starting from scratch.

Diffusion: The spreading of something widely. In the context of this work: an idea, a technology, or animals and crops.

Domestication: The intentional act of adapting plants and animals for human consumption and use.

Evolutionary biology: A field of biology that examines the origins of diversity in the natural world.

Glottochronology: The use of statistical data to date when languages diverged from their common source.

Hunter-gatherer(s): A nomadic person or people who move around in order to hunt, fish, and harvest. Their relocation depends on their ability to find food, and is often tied to the changing of the seasons, weather patterns, or the migration of animals.

Indigenous: Native or naturally occurring.

Metallurgy: The science of metals, including production and refinement.

Overkill hypothesis: A theory arguing that hunter-gatherers hunted large mammals to extinction in Australia and the Americas.

Self-catalytic: Chemical or biological progress made without a specific catalyst or intentional cause.

Critical Response

- Pulitzer Prize for General Nonfiction winner
- *New York Times* bestseller
- California Book Awards Gold Medal winner
- Phi Beta Kappa Award in Science winner
- National bestseller
- Royal Society Rhône-Poulenc Prize for Science Books Prize winner

"In its sweep, *Guns, Germs, and Steel* encompasses the rise of agriculture, technology, writing, government, and religion, providing a unifying theory of human history as intriguing as the histories of dinosaurs and glaciers." —Bill Gates

"Refuting racist explanations for presumed differences in intelligence or technological capability and eschewing a Eurocentric worldview, Diamond argues persuasively that accidental differences in geography and environment, combined with centuries of conquest, genocide and epidemics, shaped the disparate populations of today's world."

—*Publishers Weekly* (starred review)

"While you have heard many of these arguments before, Diamond has brought them together convincingly.... A fair answer to Yali's question this surely is, and gratifyingly, it makes clear that race has nothing to do with who does or does not develop cargo."

—*Kirkus Reviews*

"Diamond meshes technological mastery with historical sweep, anecdotal delight with broad conceptual vision, and command of sources with creative leaps. No finer work of its kind has been published this year, or for many past."   —*The Washington Post*

About Jared Diamond

Jared Diamond was born in Boston, MA, in 1937. His father—a pediatrician and medical researcher—inspired Diamond's interest in science; his mother—a teacher and linguist—gave him a love of reading and writing. Though Diamond began his undergraduate years at Harvard College, intending to pursue a career as a doctor, his interests shifted away from medicine and toward laboratory research. After college, Diamond received his doctorate in physiology from Cambridge. He went on to work as a researcher at Harvard Medical School before moving to California and taking a job as a physiology professor at UCLA Medical School.

Diamond began to expand his scientific focus

beyond physiology after a visit to New Guinea in 1964, where he began conducting field research on the evolution of birds. He also started publishing articles and essays in a variety of scientific publications, including *Nature* and *Discover* magazines. These writing gigs led to his first book, *The Third Chimpanzee: The Evolution and Future of the Human Animal*, which received the 1992 Royal Society Prize for Science Books. Next came *Why Is Sex Fun?: The Evolution of Human Sexuality* in 1997 and, later that same year, *Guns, Germs, and Steel,* which garnered Diamond widespread acclaim, won several major awards (including the Pulitzer Prize), sold millions of copies, was translated into more than twenty-five languages, and was featured in a documentary series on PBS.

After the success of *Guns, Germs, and Steel,* Diamond left laboratory research and devoted himself to geography, evolutionary biology, and comparative environmental history. His extensive field research includes numerous trips to New Guinea to study ecology and bird evolution—on one New Guinean trip, he rediscovered New Guinea's lost golden-fronted bowerbird. He has also gone on scientific expeditions to South America, Australia, Asia, and Africa. He is a member of the board of directors of the World Wildlife Fund USA and Conservation International. As a conservationist, Diamond created a comprehensive plan for New Guinea's national parks.

In recent years, Diamond has continued to publish journal and magazine articles as well as the book *Collapse: How Societies Choose to Fail or Succeed. Collapse* was a finalist for the Aventis Prize for Science Books and was the basis for a National Geographic documentary film.

For Your Information

Online

"Diamond in the Rough: Reflections on Guns, Germs, and Steel." HumanEcologyReview.org

"Guns, Germs and Steel: The Fates of Human Societies." C-Span.org

"Guns, Germs and Steel: Jared Diamond on Geography as Power." NationalGeographic.com

"Q&A with Jared Diamond, Author of *Guns, Germs, and Steel.*" WashingtonPost.com

"Jared Diamond: Why Do Societies Collapse?" Ted.com

"Understanding History with *Guns, Germs, and Steel.*" NPR.org

Books

1491: New Revelations of the Americas before Columbus by Charles C. Mann

After Victory: Institutions, Strategic Restraint, and the Rebuilding of Order After Major Wars by G. John Ikenberry

Arctic Dreams by Barry Lopez

Chaos by James Gleick

Cows, Pigs, Wars, & Witches: The Riddles of Culture by Marvin Harris

The Human Web: A Bird's-Eye View of World History by John Robert McNeill and William Hardy McNeill

The Memory of Fire Trilogy by Eduardo Galeano

The Sea Around Us by Rachel Carson

Scourge: The Once and Future Threat of Smallpox by Jonathan B. Tucker

Seven Elements That Have Changed the World by John Browne

A Short History of Nearly Everything by Bill Bryson

The Wealth and Poverty of Nations: Why Some Are So Rich and Some So Poor by David S. Landes

The World Without Us by Alan Weisman

Other Books by Jared Diamond

Collapse: How Societies Choose to Fail or Succeed

The Third Chimpanzee: The Evolution and Future of the Human Animal

Why Is Sex Fun?: The Evolution of Human Sexuality
The World Until Yesterday: What Can We Learn from
Traditional Societies?

Bibliography

Carey, Bjorn. "Sahara Desert Was Once Lush and Populated." *LiveScience.* July 20, 2006. Accessed September 21, 2016. http://www.livescience.com /4180-sahara-desert-lush-populated.html.

"College of Agricultural and Environmental Sciences." *UC Davis College of Agricultural and Environmental Sciences.* Accessed September 17, 2016. http://www.caes.ucdavis.edu/research/dept.

Crosby, Alfred. "Geography Is Fate: Guns, Germs, and Steel." Review of *Guns, Germs, and Steel. Los Angeles Times,* March 9, 1997.

Diamond, Jared. "About Me." JaredDiamond.com. Accessed September 17, 2016. http://www

.jareddiamond.org/Jared_Diamond/About_
Me.html.

Explorers Council. "Jared Diamond, Geographer Information, Facts, News, Photos—National Geographic." *The National Geographic.* Accessed September 17, 2016. http://www .nationalgeographic.com/explorers/bios/jared-diamond/.

Foley, William A. "Papuan Languages." *Encylopædia Britannica.* June 02, 2011. Accessed September 21, 2016. https://www.britannica.com/topic /Papuan-languages.

"The Future of Agriculture Depends on Biodiversity." FAO Newsroom. Accessed September 19, 2016. http://www.fao.org/Newsroom/en/focus/2004 /51102/index.html.

"Jared Diamond." PBS. Accessed September 17, 2016. http://www.pbs.org/gunsgermssteel/about/jared .html.

McNeill, William H. "History Upside Down." Review of *Guns, Germs, and Steel. New York Review of Books,* May 15, 1997.

Meyers, Hannah. "Suave Molecules of Mocha—Coffee, Chemistry, and Civilization." New Partisan. Accessed September 12, 2016. https://web .archive.org/web/20070221214125/http://www .newpartisan.com/home/suave-molecules-of-mocha-coffee-chemistry-and-civilization.html.

"Guns, Germs, and Steel: The Fates of Human Societies." *PublishersWeekly*. Accessed September 17, 2016. http://www.publishersweekly.com/978-0-393-03891-0.

"Pizarro Executes Last Inca Emperor." *History .com*. Accessed September 17, 2016. http://www .history.com/this-day-in-history/pizarro-executes-last-inca-emperor.

Renfrew, Colin. "Human Destinies and Ultimate Causes." Review of *Guns, Germs, and Steel*. *Nature* 386 (March 27, 1997): 339–40.

Senner, Wayne M. *The Origins of Writing*. Lincoln: University of Nebraska Press, 1991. 110–11.

"Sequoyah and the Cherokee Syllabary." Cherokee Nation: About the Nation. Accessed September 17, 2016. http://www.cherokee.org/AboutTheNation /History/Facts/SequoyahandtheCherokeeSyllabary .aspx.

Shreeve, James. "Dominance and Submission." *The New York Times*. June 15, 1997. Accessed September 16, 2016. https://www.nytimes.com/books/97 /06/15/reviews/970615.15shreevt.html.

Sieff, Martin. "Natural Forces That Shaped Human Fate." Review of *Guns, Germs, and Steel*. *The Washington Times*, May 17, 1997.

WORTH BOOKS

SMART SUMMARIES

So much to read, so little time?

Explore summaries of bestselling fiction and essential nonfiction books on a variety of subjects, including business, history, science, lifestyle, and much more.

Visit the store at
www.ebookstore.worthbooks.com

MORE SMART SUMMARIES
FROM WORTH BOOKS

HISTORY

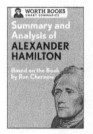

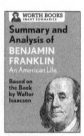

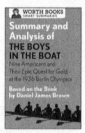

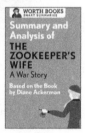

WORTH BOOKS
SMART SUMMARIES

MORE SMART SUMMARIES
FROM WORTH BOOKS

POPULAR SCIENCE

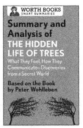

WORTH BOOKS
SMART SUMMARIES

EARLY BIRD BOOKS
FRESH EBOOK DEALS, DELIVERED DAILY

LOVE TO READ?
LOVE GREAT SALES?

GET FANTASTIC DEALS ON BESTSELLING EBOOKS DELIVERED TO YOUR INBOX EVERY DAY!

SIGN UP NOW
at www.EarlyBirdBooks.com

OPEN ROAD

INTEGRATED MEDIA

Find a full list of our authors and
titles at www.openroadmedia.com

FOLLOW US
@OpenRoadMedia

CPSIA information can be obtained
at www.ICGtesting.com
Printed in the USA
LVHW030407220720
661196LV00002B/147

Summary and Analysis of

GUNS, GERMS, AND STEEL

The Fates of Human Societies

Based on the Book by Jared Diamond

WORTH BOOKS

SMART SUMMARIES

9 781504 046572